God isn't far away;
He surrounds you
with His love...
He's in every good thing
that touches you...
in every step you make
and every breath you take.
He's not far away,
for He is with you always.

— Nancye Sims

Other Bestselling Books by
Blue Mountain Press INC.

Books by Susan Polis Schutz:
To My Daughter, with Love, on the Important Things in Life
To My Son with Love
I Love You

100 Things to Always Remember... and One Thing to Never Forget
by Alin Austin

Is It Time to Make a Change?
by Deanna Beisser

Trust in Yourself
by Donna Fargo

Too Wise to Want to Be Young Again
by Natasha Josefowitz, Ph.D.

For You, Just Because You're Very Special to Me
by Collin McCarty

Chasing Away the Clouds
by Douglas Pagels

Anthologies:
42 Gifts I'd Like to Give to You
Always Believe in Yourself and Your Dreams
Always Follow Your Dreams
Be Proud of All You've Achieved
The Best Thing in Life Is a Friend
Creeds of Life, Love, & Inspiration
Don't Ever Give Up Your Dreams
For a Special Teenager
For You, My Daughter
Friends for Life
I Love You, Mom
I Want Our Love to Last Forever
The Joys and Challenges of Motherhood
Life Can Be Hard Sometimes ...but It's Going to Be Okay
Marriage Is a Promise of Love
Mottos to Live By
Take Each Day One Step at a Time
Teaching and Learning Are Lifelong Journeys
There Is Greatness Within You, My Son
Think Positive Thoughts Every Day
Thoughts of Friendship
Thoughts of Love
To My Child
True Friends Always Remain in Each Other's Heart
Words of Love
You're Just like a Sister to Me

With God
by Your Side

...You Never
Have to Be Alone

A collection from
Blue Mountain Arts®

Edited by Gary Morris

Blue Mountain Press®

Boulder, Colorado

Library of Congress Catalog Card Number: 99-16857
ISBN: 0-88396-526-7

Poem by Susan Polis Schutz on pages 18 – 19, copyright © 1972 by Continental Publications.

ACKNOWLEDGMENTS appear on page 64.

design on book cover is registered in the U.S. Patent and Trademark Office.

Manufactured in the United States of America
First Printing in Hardcover: July 1999

This book is printed on recycled paper.

Library of Congress Cataloging-in-Publication Data

With God by your side-- you never have to be alone / edited by Gary Morris.
        p.   cm.
    ISBN 0-88396-526-7 (alk. paper)
    1. Religious poetry, American.   2. God poetry.   I. Morris, Gary,
1958-
PS595.R4W55   1999
811.008'0382--dc21   99-16857
                                                                          CIP

Blue Mountain Press INC.

P.O. Box 4549, Boulder, Colorado 80306

Contents

God Will
Take Care of You

"He Himself has said,
I will not in any way fail you
nor give you up
nor leave you without support."

Hebrews 13:5

May your heart always
find peace and comfort in the knowledge
that you are never alone.
May God's presence ease your spirit
and give you rest when you need it.
He knows how you feel.
He is ever aware of your circumstances
and ready to be your strength,
your grace, and your peace.

He is there to cast sunlight
into all of your darkened shadows,
to send encouragement through the love
of friends and family, and
to replace your weariness with new hope.
God is your stronghold,
and with Him as your guide,
you need never be afraid.
No circumstances can block His love.
No grief is too hard for Him to bear.
No task is too difficult
for Him to complete.
When what you are feeling
is simply too deep for words
and nothing anyone does or says
can provide you with the relief you need,
God understands.
He is your provider —
today, tomorrow, and always.
And He loves you.
Cast all of your cares on Him...
    and believe.

— Linda E. Knight

When One Door Closes
in Our Lives,
God Always Opens Another

Sometimes when we
least expect it,
a door closes in our lives.
Circumstances may change,
dreams may get shattered,
and plans for tomorrow
may disappear.
But when one door closes,
   God always opens another.

When we're facing disappointment
  in our lives,
sometimes it's hard to see
that this is also part of God's plan —
but it's true.
God knows what is best for us,
and He will lead us
to where we need to be.

Have faith in Him,
and you will reach
all the wondrous things
that He has waiting for you.

— B. L. McDaniel

What God Promises

He doesn't promise sunny days;
just a rainbow at the end of a storm.

He doesn't promise silver and gold,
but to provide for your needs.

He doesn't promise to make
    your life trouble free,
just to give you the strength
    to see things through.

He doesn't promise all the answers,
just that He'll direct your path.

He doesn't promise you understanding,
but faith that will see you through.

He doesn't promise freedom
    from despair,
only joy and peace in believing.

He doesn't promise that
    you'll never fail,
just that your strength and hope
    will be renewed.

He doesn't promise
    you'll have no fears,
but that He is always there.

Most of all, He promises
    unconditional and everlasting
        love.

— Barbara Cage

Have Faith

Faith is the answer
to every doubt, every fear,
and every question.
Faith assures you that you can
and you will.

— Donna Newman

Where there is faith,
there is love;
Where there is love,
there is peace;
Where there is peace,
there is God;
Where there is God,
there is no need.

— Leo Tolstoy

Faith isn't anything you can see;
it isn't anything you can touch.
But you can feel it in your heart.
Faith is what keeps you trying
when others would have given up.
It keeps you believing in
the goodness of others
and helps you find it.
Faith is trusting in a power
greater than yourself
and knowing that whatever happens,
this power will carry you through
anything.
It is believing in yourself
and having the courage
to stand up for what you believe in.
Faith is
peace in the midst of a storm,
determination in the midst
of adversity,
and safety in the midst of trouble.
For nothing can touch a soul
that is protected by faith.

— Barbara Cage

God Is Never
Far Away

God isn't far away;
He surrounds you
with His love.
It was He who opened
your eyes this morning.
It is His strength
that will carry you
through this day,
and it is in His peace
that your heart will
find rest tonight.

God isn't far away.
He is the light of this day.
He is the sky above you,
the earth beneath you,
and the life of every living thing.

He is in every smile,
in every thought that gives you hope,
in every tear that waters your soul,
and in every moment you can't
face alone.

He's the love on your loved one's face.
He's in the friends along the way —
in strangers you have yet to meet
and blessings you have yet to receive.

He's in every good thing
that touches you.
He is in every step you make
and every breath you take.
He's not far away,
for He is with you always.

— Nancye Sims

"A Little Prayer"

May you have a little sunlight
to guide you on your way.
May you discover, little by little,
happiness that's here to stay.
May you grow a little stronger
and a little wiser with each dawn.
May you have a little time to
believe in dreams to dream upon.
May all the joy your heart desires
find its way to you.

And may the blessings that
brighten up your days
keep on shining through!

— Carey Martin

We need to feel more
to understand others
We need to love more
to be loved back
We need to cry more
to cleanse ourselves
We need to laugh more
to enjoy ourselves

We need to establish the values
   of honesty and fairness
when interacting with people
We need to establish
   a strong ethical basis
as a way of life

We need to see more
other than our own little fantasies
We need to hear more
and listen to the needs of others

We need to give more
and take less
We need to share more
and own less
We need to realize
   the importance of the family
as a backbone to stability
We need to look more
and realize that we are not
   so different from one another

We need to create a world where
we can all peacefully live
the life we choose
We need to create a world where
we can trust each other

— Susan Polis Schutz

Three Qualities of
a Faith-Filled Life

Transformation

Life has the potential for endless change
and growth — and faith and hope are
always available to guide you. Remember
that life has its cycles just like the
seasons, that success is planted like a
seed in every failure, and that within
every ending is a new beginning.

Sacrifice

Achieving your greatest dreams and
highest ideals may call upon you to
sacrifice your time, your talents, and
sometimes even your way of looking at
the world. Weigh these sacrifices carefully;
if the reward is worth the effort, go after
it wholeheartedly. However it turns out,
never regret the investments you make in
your dreams. Something good will always
come of them.

And most of all...

Love

Have love not only for others, but for
yourself as well. As a gift, compassion is
one of the best and most widely needed
in the world. Remember that love has the
power to create and sustain life, dreams,
and happiness; it forgives everything and
remembers nothing except the best; and it
lasts forever.

— Edmund O'Neill

A Blessing to Take with You Through the Day

Get the most you can out of life.
Know: you're in the heart of a friend.
When it comes to making dreams come
true, the special part is to simply begin.

Realize it's never too late for anything.
Each challenge is one you'll get through.
Be sure to choose the path you walk
    instead of letting it choose you.

Find serenity in everyday living.
Envision the gift of this day.
When happiness comes to visit you,
    encourage it to stay.

Realize: there's a very special someone
you can count on to be a friend.
Something people see when they look
at you is the beautiful person within.

Trust your heart to guide you.
Keep your soul beside you in everything.
Meet each day's tests.
And know that you're wished
    every success that life can bring.

— Douglas Pagels

Visualize in your mind,
even for a few moments,
what success would look like to you.
See yourself somewhere in that vision
as content and happy.
You can achieve whatever you want
as long as you have faith
and believe that you deserve
what God intended for you.
Visualize what it is that you want,
then work toward it;
take one step each day.
Half the battle is won
if you just keep that vision
firmly planted in your life.
The rest is in the hands of God.

— Sherrie L. Householder

Remember That Change
Is a Natural Part
of All Life

Clouds do not stand still
Trees bloom, then shed their leaves
Tides come to shore, then retreat
Night follows day
which in turn follows night
Life is a constant cycle
ever changing
yet never changing
and we are a part of it all
We will be here for a time
but only until our time is done
We have only just so much time
to make our mark
so that we are worth remembering
We should realize that we
are as important
as the clouds, the tides
   and the seasons
We have our place
and must play our part
as best we can
in life's ever—unfolding story

— Rhoda-Katie Hannan

God Knows...

When you are tired
and discouraged from
fruitless efforts...
God knows how hard
you have tried.
When you've cried so long
and your heart is in anguish...
God has counted your tears.
If you feel that your life
is on hold
and time has passed you by...
God is waiting with you.
When you're lonely
and your friends are too busy
even for a phone call...
God is by your side.
When you think you've tried everything
and don't know where to turn...
God has a solution.
When nothing makes sense
and you are confused
or frustrated...
God has the answer.

If suddenly your outlook is brighter
and you find traces of hope...
God has whispered to you.
When things are going well
and you have much to be
thankful for...
God has blessed you.
When something joyful happens
and you are filled with awe...
God has smiled upon you.
When you have a purpose to fulfill
and a dream to follow...
God has opened your eyes
and called you by name.
Remember that wherever you are
or whatever you're facing...
God knows.

— Kelly D. Caron

May God Fill Your Heart with Hope

Hope is a word that
every hurting heart understands.
Hope shines brighter
    than the darkest night.
Faith is bigger
    than the highest mountain.
And God is greater
    than any obstacle
        in your path.

Anything can be accomplished
    by those who
fully put their hearts into it.
The time to start is now;
the place to start is here.

May hope cast its special light
    upon your path
and God bless everything you touch
    in the hours, days,
        and moments still to come.

— Linda E. Knight

Remember What It Means to Have the Lord in Your Life

Having the Lord in your life means that you have peace and comfort in your heart as you walk down any pathway your life has to offer.

It means you can pray to a caring and compassionate Father who always has the time to listen and who never fails to understand the hurts and fears that are dwelling in the depths of your soul.

Having the Lord in your life means having the assurance that nothing can ever come your way that you and He, united together, cannot deal with and ultimately overcome. Even though tears, hurts, and painful times have come and undoubtedly will continue to come, you can know that He has His hand in everything, and things will always work out for your good.

It means that you can be assured, with no uncertainty, that you will be given the strength to endure anything that happens to you, and you will become a better person.

Even though all of these blessings are crucial to our day-to-day existence on this earth, they are small compared to the promise of spending an eternity in His presence.

Therefore, what it means to have the Lord in your life is knowing the blessed hope of tomorrow and the glorious promise of heaven that He has prepared for us!

— Cathy Beddow Keener

The Power of Prayer
Will Light Your Way

Prayer is so simple.
It is like quietly opening a door
And slipping into
The very presence of God.
There, in the stillness,
To listen for His voice,
Perhaps in petition
Or only to listen,
It matters not.
Just to be there,
In His presence,
Is prayer.

— Anonymous

More things are wrought by prayer
Than this world dreams of.

— Alfred, Lord Tennyson

"Dear Lord..."

May my heart
be your temple
May my words
be your song
May you dwell
inside me all
the day long
May my eyes see your glory; may my breath take you in
May you always be with me to deliver me from my sins
May my ears hear your whispers as you watch me sleep
May I always see the path you have lighted for my feet
May I have peace
and convey your
wishes to others
May I regard any
stranger as if he
were my brother
May I always love
you and obey all
of your commands
May you always be
my Savior who
forever holds my hand.

— Kendra D. Elmore

I Prayed for You Today

I prayed for you today, gave thanks for your life, wished you the best, asked the heavens to bless you with good health and happiness. I sent you good thoughts, surrounded you with hope and faith and love. I asked your guardian angels to protect you and keep you safe from any harm and to blanket you with joy and contentment and peace and prosperity.

I prayed for you today. I asked that you be guided with the wisdom to make choices to enhance your life and the awareness to make changes that are in your best interest. I wished for you a storehouse of opportunities, the ability to meet your goals, and the joy of your own approval and acceptance. I wished for you your heart's desire, every need met, every prayer answered, and every dream come true.

I prayed for you today. I asked that you be prepared for whatever life hands you or whatever you're going through. I asked that your spirit be strong and lead you and guide you each step of the way down every path you take. I asked the universe to confirm for you that you're someone very special. I asked the earth to be good to you, and I asked God to show you His perfect way. I prayed for you today.

— Donna Fargo

It's hard for us to accept the fact that our priorities are not the same as God's. We attach too much importance to things like popularity, wealth, and political success. To Him problems that often seem most important to us at the time are really not very significant. But God trusts us to make the best use of the time we have... and to make our lives meaningful and beneficial to others no matter where we are.

— Jimmy Carter

To everything there is a season,
A time for every purpose
under Heaven.

— Ecclesiastes 3:1

Come to Me, all you who labor and are heavy laden, and I will give you rest.

— Matthew 11:28

I had learned many years ago to release my problems to God, something I had to do often in all our political years when I was trying to do so many different things at once. "Here it is, God. You take it. I can't handle it alone," I would say. It helped me through the good times and the bad. I knew that God loved me. I had found God's love a shield around me in the midst of controversy or letdowns.

— Rosalynn Carter

Enjoy the blessings of this day, if God sends them, and the evils of it bear patiently and sweetly; for this day only is ours; we are dead to yesterday, and we are not born to the morrow. He, therefore, that enjoys the present, if it be good, enjoys as much as is possible; and if only that day's trouble leans upon him, it is singular and finite.

When a storm of a sad mischance beats upon our spirits, turn it into some advantage by observing where it can serve another end of more safety or less envy: it will turn into something that is good, if we list to make it so; at least it may make us weary of the world's vanity and take off our confidence from uncertain riches and make our spirits to dwell in those regions where content dwells essentially. If it does any good to our souls, it hath made more than sufficient recompense for all the temporal affliction.

— Jeremy Taylor

This is the day
which the Lord has made;
We will rejoice
and be glad in it.

— Psalm 118:24

Be glad of life, because it gives you the chance to love and to work and to play and to look up at the stars; to think often of your friends, and every day of Christ; and to spend as much time as you can, with body and with spirit, in God's out-of-doors.

These are the little guideposts on the footpath to peace.

— Henry van Dyke

Trust in God...
He Always Guides Us

When life seems to fall down around us,
   it is comforting to know
that we don't have to
   carry our burdens alone.
God will guide us
   through the darkest days.

Sometimes, it is difficult to trust that
   what we are going through at the moment
      will work out for the best.
But God has a way of helping us
   learn from the bad
      in order to prepare us for the good.

This simple act of trusting God
   can take us to a different level
      of peace and understanding...
         and away from fear and uncertainty.
Even when you feel that
   the weight of the world is on you,
never lose faith in your determination
   to redirect your life...
so that you can
   continue your journey
      to the best of your ability.

— Elizabeth Hornsey Reeves

The Faith You Can Depend On

Sometimes it's hard to keep your faith
when life turns your world upside down.
But a foundation built on
    God's promises
is a faith you can depend on.

Sometimes, just reaching out to God
brings the peace and strength you need
to stand up, speak out, and take charge
when life turns your world upside down.

Because you're special to God
and building your foundation on Him,
He'll supply all of your needs
and give you a rainbow of hope.

When things get in the way
of living a life that counts,
remember to do a little soul searching
and spend quiet time with God.
He'll supply you with inner peace
and give you the strength
to build an even stronger foundation.
If you stand on His promises,
it is and always will be
the faith you can depend on.

— Edward O'Blenis

God Gives Us Friends
to Help Us Through
the Difficult Times

God gave us the seasons —
   each with its own beauty and reason,
      each meant to bring us a blessing,
         a joy, and a feeling of love.
God gave us dreams —
   each with its own secret,
      each sent to give us feelings of
         inspiration, hope, and tranquility.
God gave us the sunshine,
   the rainbows and the rain,
      the beauty and freedom of nature
to teach us the wisdom of gentle acceptance.
God gave us miracles
   in our hearts and lives,
      little things that happen
         to remind us we're alive.

God gave us the ability
   to face each new day
      with courage, wisdom,
         and a smile from knowing
that whatever sorrow or pain we face,
   He abides with us
      securely in our hearts.
Most of all, God gave us friends
   to teach us about love
      and guide us through this world,
always available to help us forward
   toward a greater understanding
      and a greater sharing and giving
         of love.

— Regina Hill

How to Be
an Earthbound Guardian Angel

Be a friend; true friendship is a
   priceless gift.
Always listen with your heart; you
   must listen to a person before you
   can attempt to help them in any
   way, so always listen wholeheartedly.
Reach out to those in need, even if you
   aren't quite sure what it is that they
   need from you.
Realize that miracles are not mysterious
   or impossible to achieve. A miracle is
   the small thing you do that makes a
   big difference in someone else's life.
Remind someone that life is precious
   and worth living, even though their
   world seems hopeless and dark.

Know that feeling is the key to understanding. You must have some idea of how the other person feels before you can begin to understand them.

Keep the spirit of the holidays with you all year long. Don't pack away your good will along with the ornaments after the holidays.

Be honest in loving and caring about someone; sincere compassion is the best kind to give, and honesty is angelic.

Don't expect to sprout wings; instead, be satisfied with the warm flutter of accomplishment.

Listen to your intuition; it won't fail you in times of doubt.

Most of all, encourage more people to do all of the above, through your own shining example.

— Connie Anzalone

I asked God for strength, that I
might achieve —
I was made weak, that I might learn
humbly to obey.

I asked for health, that I might
do greater things —
I was given infirmity, that I might
do better things.

I asked for riches, that I might be happy —
I was given poverty, that I might be wise.

I asked for power, that I might have the
praise of men —
I was given weakness, that I might
feel the need of God.

I asked for all things, that I might
  enjoy life —
I was given life, that I might
  enjoy all things.

I got nothing that I asked for —
  but everything I had hoped for.

Almost despite myself, my unspoken prayers
  were answered.

I am, among all people, most richly blessed!

— Anonymous

Lord, just for today, help me:

Give more and take less,
   and always give something back;
Take responsibility for myself
   and don't place blame on
   or wait for others;
Live with integrity and courage,
   with an eye to the future of us all;
Look at the world and think
   "This is ours,"
   not "This is mine";
Ask how I can help and what I can contribute,
   instead of how much more I can have;
Look out of windows
   instead of staring into mirrors,
   and see past the narrow confines of myself;

Act with compassion and tolerance
in all things and to everyone;
Know that sometimes mine isn't the only way,
but only one more way to try;
Live in harmony with this earth
and treasure all its gifts;
Try to understand more
and therefore fear less,
accept more and judge less,
love more and hate less;
To know that it's up to me
to start today to give back
more than I take;
To pass on the magnificent wonders
of this earth to my children
and to their children.

— Vickie M. Worsham

Love lights up
the world and makes
our troubles
seem insignificant
Love is God's
most magnificent gift

— Joanne Bragdonne

How Much Does God Love You?

Do you ever look up
to see the stars at night?
Have you tried to count them all
or imagine their number,
feeling small and insignificant
and overwhelmed at the sight?

Do you ever try to picture
the Hand that put
each star in its place,
that knows their number,
and — more importantly —
knows that you are looking up
to see the vastness
of His universe?
He sees your face,
hears your thoughts,
and reads your heart.

God loves you more than
    all the stars in heaven.
There's an endless amount of love
    that He is always sending you,
and His love is there to cover
    every moment of your life.

— Barbara J. Hall

You're a Special Person in God's Eyes

On the day you were born...
God held the stars
Within His hands
And watched as they twinkled
    and shined.
He tried to find two
    of the best He observed,
But He couldn't quite make up
    His mind.
Then suddenly two of them
    danced in the air,
And the rest of them
    took to the skies.
On the day you were born,
You were blessed with the stars
    that were chosen
To shine in your eyes.

— Desirée Derosier-Kaczor

Someone's Watching
Over You

Someone's watching over you
   with the greatest love.
Someone wants you to be
   happy, safe, and secure;
Someone considers you
   a wonderful individual
   and cares about your needs.

Someone's making blessings
   for your benefit right now —
like sunshine for those rainy days
and rainbows to remind you
   of the promise up ahead.

Someone's watching over you
   especially today.
And He will take
   good care of you.

— Barbara J. Hall

55

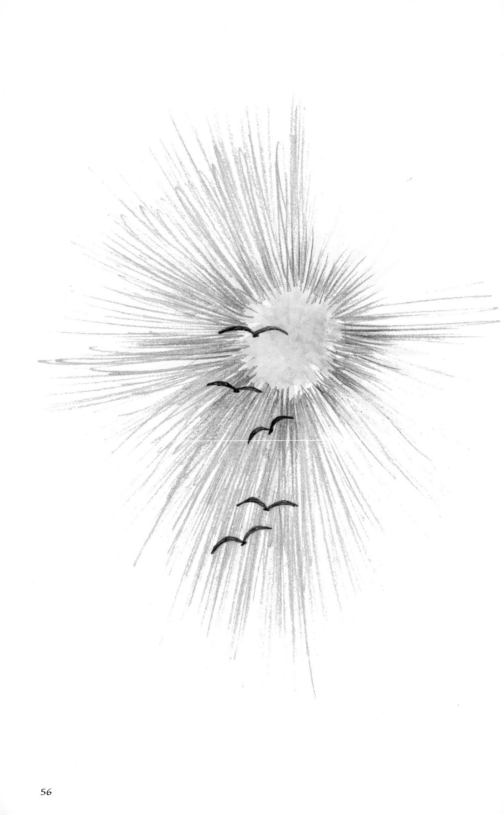

Expect a Miracle!

Miracles can and do happen. They can come at any time. Even when things seem darkest, there is a miracle lurking nearby.

Believing in the impossible, even when the obvious is staring you in the face, produces extraordinary results. The darkest cloud produces the brightest light when the sun breaks through. Believing in the sun, even though you can't see it, is what faith is all about.

God knows when the impossible is just about to get you down, and He needs to let you know how much He cares. That's when He gives you the miracle you've been looking for. In that moment, the clouds part and the sun will come through for you.

— Rodger Austin

God Gives You
a Rainbow
for Every Rainy Day

Often, it is through
the most difficult days of our lives
that we come to know ourselves
and what is truly most important to us.
No matter how sad you may feel at times,
be confident that hope will
awaken with you tomorrow.
Faith and courage reach out to you;
take hold of them, and you will find
that you will be able to smile again
and truly be happy once more.

How we deal with life
is really a matter of personal choice,
so choose to be happy.
Find joy in the simplest things,
and see beauty in each person you meet.
When times are difficult,
remind yourself that no pain
comes to you without a purpose.
Above all, trust in
God's handcrafted plan
that He has made just for you.
Let Him love you through life's
joyous and painful aspects;
if you do,
you will find inner peace
and unending joy.

— Kelly Wolfe

Believe in Angels

There's an angel
always by your side.

Whether male or female,
it's there to be your guide.

It rejoices with each sunrise,
the beginning of each day,
knowing that you're safe, indeed,
for in God's hands you stay.

And when the evening comes
and the darkness makes its cover,
your angel settles
   in the coming night
and above your head it hovers.

Believe in angels —
you have your very own,
because you are God's special child
and you'll never be alone.

— Barbara Cage

May You Be
with God,
for God Is Always
with You

You are not alone. You never have been, and you never will be. God has been with you every step of the way. Where the path leads, He is lighting lamps to guide you.

And if you ever do feel for a second that He is not right there beside you, it is only because He has gone ahead for a moment or two to build a bridge that will keep you safe from harm and that will lead you on toward the sunlight shining through.

Wherever you go, may you be with God, for God will always be with you.

— Alin Austin

With God by Your Side,
You Never Have to Be Alone

Sometimes life sends us
changes we've never contemplated,
problems we'd just as soon do without,
and inconveniences that we'd rather not
    have to deal with.
It can feel as if we are wandering
    in a barren desert.

It's during these "desert" experiences
    of our lives
that God, in all His faithfulness,
    opens up His heart.

He quenches our thirsty souls,
revives our parched hearts,
and leads us to a higher place
where peace and joy and love
    will be ours forever.

On all the long journeys
your life leads you on,
please remember...

    you'll never walk alone.

— Linda E. Knight

Acknowledgments

We gratefully acknowledge the permission granted by the following authors, publishers, and authors' representatives to reprint poems or excerpts from their publications.

PrimaDonna Entertainment Corp. for "I Prayed for You Today" by Donna Fargo. Copyright © 1999 by PrimaDonna Entertainment Corp. All rights reserved. Reprinted by permission.

University of Arkansas Press for "I had learned many years ago..." and "It's hard for us to accept the fact that..." from EVERYTHING TO GAIN by Jimmy and Rosalynn Carter. Copyright © 1987, 1995 by Jimmy Carter and Rosalynn Carter. All rights reserved. Reprinted by permission.

Barbara Cage for "What God Promises." Copyright © 1998 by Barbara Cage. All rights reserved. Reprinted by permission.

Sherrie L. Householder for "Visualize in your mind...." Copyright © 1998 by Sherrie L. Householder. All rights reserved. Reprinted by permission.

Rhoda–Katie Hannan for "Remember That Change Is a Natural Part of All Life." Copyright © 1998 by Rhoda–Katie Hannan. All rights reserved. Reprinted by permission.

Linda E. Knight for "May God Fill Your Heart with Hope." Copyright © 1998 by Linda E. Knight. All rights reserved. Reprinted by permission.

Kendra D. Elmore for "Dear Lord...." Copyright © 1999 by Kendra D. Elmore. All rights reserved. Reprinted by permission.

Elizabeth Hornsey Reeves for "Trust in God... He Always Guides Us." Copyright © 1999 by Elizabeth Hornsey Reeves. All rights reserved. Reprinted by permission.

Edward O'Blenis for "The Faith You Can Depend On." Copyright © 1999 by Edward O'Blenis. All rights reserved. Reprinted by permission.

Connie Anzalone for "How to Be an Earthbound Guardian Angel." Copyright © 1998 by Connie Anzalone. All rights reserved. Reprinted by permission.

Barbara J. Hall for "How Much Does God Love You?" and "Someone's Watching Over You." Copyright © 1998 by Barbara J. Hall. All rights reserved. Reprinted by permission.

Vickie M. Worsham for "Lord, just for today, help me...." Copyright © 1998 by Vickie M. Worsham. All rights reserved. Reprinted by permission.

Desirée Derosier–Kaczor for "You're a Special Person in God's Eyes." Copyright © 1998 by Desirée Derosier–Kaczor. All rights reserved. Reprinted by permission.

Rodger Austin for "Expect a Miracle!" Copyright © 1998 by Rodger Austin. All rights reserved. Reprinted by permission.

The Scripture quotation on page 4 is from the Amplified New Testament, © 1954, 1958, 1987 by the Lockman Foundation. Used by permission. Scripture quotations on pages 36, 37, and 39 are from the New King James Version. Copyright © 1979, 1980, 1982 by Thomas Nelson, Inc. All rights reserved. Reprinted by permission.

A careful effort has been made to trace the ownership of poems used in this anthology in order to obtain permission to reprint copyrighted materials and give proper credit to the copyright owners. If any error or omission has occurred, it is completely inadvertent, and we would like to make corrections in future editions provided that written notification is made to the publisher:

BLUE MOUNTAIN PRESS, INC., P.O. Box 4549, Boulder, Colorado 80306.